NEWTON PAGE

TWO OVERTURES

HUMBLY OFFERED TO HIS GRACE JOHN DUKE OF ARGYLL, HER MAJESTIES HIGH COMMISSIONER, AND THE RIGHT HONOURABLE THE ESTATES OF PARLIAMENT.

By

John Law

(1705)

Edited by

Gavin John Adams

NEWTON PAGE

NEWTON PAGE

www.newtonpage.com

Two Overtures

Humbly offered to his Grace JOHN Duke of ARGYLL, Her Majesties High Commissioner, and the Right Honourable the Estates of Parliament.

By

John Law

Edited by
Gavin John Adams

Published by Newton Page 2021

1 3 5 7 9 10 8 6 4 2

ISBN 978-1-934619-23-0
Library of Congress Control Number: 2021930045

Published in the United States of America, Louisville, KY.
Set in Adobe Garamond Pro

CONTENTS

NOTE ON THE TEXT

Since *Two Overtures Humbly offered to his Grace JOHN Duke of ARGYLL, Her Majesties High Commissioner, and the right Honourable the Estates of Parliament* was first published in the early eighteenth-century, conventions of spelling, grammar, punctuation, expression, vocabulary and general notation have each undergone considerable modernization. In addition, the relatively crude practices of eighteenth-century book and pamphlet production have been gradually replaced by the radically more exacting standards of modern publishing, which demand both uniformity of typesetting and editorial consistency. As a consequence of those changes, the modern reader is used to a more polished product than those available in the past.

However, notwithstanding the usual expectations of the modern reader, and in full appreciation that the original texts are not as easy on the modern eye as they would have been on their contemporary equivalents, the temptation to edit them to conform with modern writing and publishing conventions has been largely resisted. That approach has been taken because to do anything other than retain the original form of the texts would be to detract from their character. The only two minor exceptions to that approach have been the correction of dischordant italics and the replacement of the medial s with the modern s.

The pamphlet was both written and published for the consideration of John Campbell, 2nd Duke of Argyll and those interested in the macro-economic development of Scotland. As such, it is tailored to conform with the conventional eighteenth-century stylistic expectations of that readership. American readers will notice that in maintaining the integrity of the original publications, the original historic British forms of spelling have been retained. More generally, readers will notice both inconsistent and imaginative forms of spelling throughout.

Reproduced in this book is the first edition and printing of:

Two Overtures Humbly offered to his Grace JOHN Duke of ARGYLL, Her Majesties High Commissioner, and the right Honourable the Estates of Parliament (1705).

TWO

OVERTURES

Humbly offered to his Grace *JOHN* Duke of *ARGYLL*, Her Majesties High Commissioner, and the right Honourable the Estates of Parliament.

TWO OVERTURES

HUMBLY OFFERED TO HIS GRACE JOHN DUKE OF ARGYLL, HER MAJESTIES HIGH COMMISSIONER, AND THE RIGHT HONOURABLE THE ESTATES OF PARLIAMENT.

TWO OVERTURES

HUMBLY OFFERED TO HIS GRACE JOHN DUKE OF ARGYLL, HER MAJESTIES HIGH COMMISSIONER, AND THE RIGHT HONOURABLE THE ESTATES OF PARLIAMENT.

The I. For Supplying the present Scarcity of Coyn, and, Improving Trade.

The 2. For clearing the Debts due by the Government to the Army and Civil List.

There need no Speeches to shew how much a sufficient Stock of Money, or a good Fund of Publick Credit, which is the same thing, (Money being but the Counter in Commerce) would be serviceable to the People and Trade of the Kingdom; or how much it would tend to the Honour, and Justice of the Queen and Parliament. To pay off, and clear the Debts of the Government; so long and so justly due to the Army and Civil List.

'Tis the part of every Subject, to seek the Ease and Honour of the Government; and the Good and Prosperity of his Countrey: He who has the Happiness by his Indeavours, to do Service to either, deserves to be encouraged by both, and even he who fails in his Attempt, having done his best, merits the Thanks of these to whom he has shewed his good Wishes.

OVERTURE I.

For supplying the present Scarcity of Coyn, and improving Trade.

OVERTURE I.

FOR SUPPLYING THE PRESENT SCARCITY OF COYN, AND IMPROVING TRADE.

OVERTURE I.

FOR SUPPLYING THE PRESENT SCARCITY OF COYN, AND IMPROVING TRADE.

I. That the Parliament constitute a Commission of Trade, of 30 in Number at least, of which one half to be able and knowing Merchants, the other Nobility and Barons; with power to strick such a Number of Notes bearing 3 per Cent Interest; as shall be judged the immediat Demand of Trade.

2. That these Notes so struck shall have a Parliamentary currency.

3. That the Commission of Trade have power to constitute Sub-commissions and Factors, where they please, at Home or Abroad.

4. That the Commission of Trade do imploy these Notes so struck, in erecting a Fisherie; and in improving our Manufactories: In a word, that they be imploy'd, in setting the People of the Nation to work on all things to which they can apply themselves; by buying up their Goods with these Notes, and sending them abroad, and there selling them to the best

advantage, and making such returns, as is most saleable to the Country, to be retailed here for these Notes again, or such Commodities as the Nation affords: For in such a Commission of Trade, Barter will be as good as Money.

5. That the Interest of these Notes be pay'd at the end of every half year, in Silver or Gold by the Commission of Trade; out of the first and readiest of the Profits.

6. That one Moitie of the neat Profit (the Interest of the Notes being deduced out of it) be given yearly to the Commissioners for their Service and Incouragement.

7. That the other Moitie of the neat Profit be yearly laid up in a National Stock or Treasure, by which in time all these Notes, may not only be cancell'd and pay'd off, but immense Sums kept in Bank; the whole People imploy'd, and the Nation put upon an equal Foot with its Neighbours, not only in Riches, but in Naval and Land Force.

8. That this Commission be obliged to sell all Foreign Commodities, to the Home Consumption, at 10 per Cent neat profit upon the Export.

9. These Notes may be struck from 20 shil. to 100 lib. sterling.

I am sensible a great many Objections may be raised against this Overture, but the strongest of them are so insignificant, that they are no sooner heard, than answer'd; The principal ones may be.

I. That this would be too great a Trust in the Hands of so few Men.

2. That it would ruine a great many privat Merchants.

and bring the whole Profit of the Trade to the State in general.

3. That it would take out the small Quantity of Gold and Silver we have from amongst us, at least make it of less Value than the Notes, because the Notes would be an equal Tender in Law, and bear 3 per Cent Interest.

4. That here is not a Species of so small a Dividend, as can answer the Ends of the common People, in buying up the small Necessaries they have occasion for.

As to the first Objection, That this would be too great a Trust in the hands of so few Men.

It is answered,

That the Commission is constitute by Parliament, and are accomptable, they and their Books to Parliament; They may be changed by Parliament and subjected to their Books to Parliament; They may be changed by Parliament, and subjected to such Rules, and Auditors, as not to leave it in their power to cheat the Nation of Sixpence; Or import any Commodities that are not judged necessary and useful to the People, or convenient in Trade; tho indeed it is not the Import but the Home Consumption of Forreign Goods, which should be prohibite in a well regulat State.

As to the 2d Obj. That it would ruine a great many privat Merchants, and bring the whole profit of Trade to the State in general.

'Tis answered, Grant it did; Is not the good of a State in general, preferable to the Interest of a few privat Men? But on the contrary, the Merchant would be so far from being a loser, that he's be a Gainer; for by this he'd get his Debts pay'd in, his Goods sold off, his Credit increased from the Inlargement of common tale, and might buy and send abroad such Goods or Commodities as the Commission of Trade should send Abroad; and make such Returns as are allowable in the Nation; Or if he be a Retailer, he may buy and retail from the Commission. Only this indeed it would do, it would keep the Merchants from laying exorbitant Prices upon their Goods, thereby often breaking the Landed-men, and becoming themselves the Landlords.

As to the 3d. Objection. That it would take out the small Quantity of Gold and Silver we have from amongst us; or make it of less value than the Notes.

I answer, To the last part of the Objection I agree, and it is undoubtedly our advantage; and as to the first part, it is so far from holding good; that what is here proposed, becomes immediat Cure for our want of Money, by supplying us with the Goods of the Nation to pay our Ballance Abroad; which are become due to our Neighbours, and daily growing upon our hand, by the want of a Money or Credit to imploy our People, whereby the several Products of the Country might be manufactured and exported, so as to make our Industry at Home, prevail as much against our Luxury from Abroad in time coming, as that and our neglect of Trade, has prevailed against our Coin in time past.

And as for the Fourth Objection, The Money we have yet amongst us, brought to an equal Standard with out Neighbours, would certainly be sufficient to serve our Poor, and Silver and Gold would of course increase amongst us; to what ever Value we can bring the Ballance of Trade on our side.

This indeed is no more, than the Nation lending its Faith to all its privat Subjects, and multiplying its own Credit, within it self, by which it may at any time under a well regulate Trade, imploy what Stock it has a mind to; and the greater the Stock is, that the Nation is capable to imploy, the greater our Profit, and the greater the Ballance of Trade on our side. And the sooner this Kingdom will grow great and considerable amongst its Neighbours.

Thus it was the East-India-Company in England have made themselves a vast Stock, by borrowing Money on their Bonds; which they pay'd on the return of Goods, and made the profit their own.

OVERTURE II.

For clearing the Debts due by the Government to the Army and civil Lift.

The Debts of the Government to the Army and Military Service, will be about 100000 *Sterling.*

OVERTURE II.

FOR CLEARING THE DEBTS DUE BY THE GOVERNMENT TO THE ARMY AND CIVIL LIST.

THE DEBTS OF THE GOVERNMENT TO THE ARMY AND MILITARY SERVICE, WILL BE ABOUT 100000 STERLING.

OVERTURE II.

FOR CLEARING THE DEBTS DUE BY THE GOVERNMENT TO THE ARMY AND CIVIL LIST.

THE DEBTS OF THE GOVERNMENT TO THE ARMY AND MILITARY SERVICE, WILL BE ABOUT 100000 STERLING.

I. That there be 100000 lib. struck in 5, 10, 20, & 50 lib. Sterling Notes, Debentures or Talleys (for they are all one on the matter,) bearing 3 per Cent. Interest, to be pay'd every half year at the Treasury Office, by one appointed to that purpose, and accountable to Parliament.

2. That these Notes be Issued out with a Parliamentary currency, for clearing the Debt due to the Army, as the same shall be adjusted by the Commissioners of Accompts.

3. That there be an Act of Parliament setling 14 days Cess to be payed yearly at two Terms, for satisfying the Interest of the above 100000 lib. at 3 per Cent. and that to continue till the Parliament shall lay on a Fund for sinking the principal Sum.

4. That at any time when the Interest is a paying, such Notes as are wore or tore, shall be renew'd to the Bearer, at the sight of the Lords of the Treasury, or whom else the Parliament shall think fit to appoint.

By granting this, which will only Cost the Nation 3000 lib. and pay'd within itself, and but half the Interest of its just Debt, the Army, which has been so long kept in Arrear, to the inexpressible hardship of a great many worthy Gentlemen, who served honestly for their Pay, and whose Friends and Relations are now sitting in the House, will not only be satisfy'd, if the Government designe either to pay or be owing: But these Notes, Debentures or Tallys having their Interests punctually pay'd, every half year, will circulate amongst the People, and serve in Payment equal to 100000 lib. in Gold and Silver, and be preferable in acceptance, because of the continued Interest, which at this Juncture would Advance the whole Nation six times the 14 days Cess by augmenting so much the circular Credit, and consequently the Trade thereof.

The same Measures may be taken for clearing the Debts due to the civil List, by giving out Talleys, Debentures or Notes on the Customs & Queens Revenues, so far as to satisfie the Debt; and these too to bear no more than 3 per Cent. Interest, and be sunk as the Revenue comes in: this would not only pay off those who have a just Claim under the Faith of the Government, but circulate amongst the People, and so become assisting to the Credit of the Nation.

I know it will be Objected here, That this would too far anticipate the Queens Rents, and postpone the payment of her immediat Servants; but if these will but Love their Neighbours as themselves, they'll soon Answer their own Objection, and find, that those who served first, should be first pay'd: besides, Court Service is not so certain now a days, at least amongst us, but that it were the Interest of those who have that Honour, to be once upon a Foot, by which they may be assured of their Sallaries or Pensions, at one time or other.

These two Overtures are plain and easie to be understood, the consequence visible, and in a great measure proven to good effect, in our Neighbour Nation, when they were burden'd with a heavy War, and labour'd under the almost total suppression of Coyn, when their Clipt and Brimigem Money was call'd in, and Miln'd Money only allow'd of, of which, there was but a very small Sum amongst them: But how far they'll serve us, or how far we are capable of being served by them, The Lord of Heaven knows.

FINIS.

ALSO AVAILABLE FROM NEWTON PAGE

ALSO AVAILABLE FROM NEWTON PAGE

John Law

The Lauriston Lecture and Collected Writings

Gavin John Adams

ISBN-13: 978-1-934619155

A collection of six unique accounts of the extraordinary life of John Law of Lauriston and the operation of his infamous Mississippi Scheme. In addition to the first lecture on the life of John Law to be delivered at Law's ancestral home of Lauriston Castle, also included in this collection are accounts of his life and the Mississippi Scheme by some of the most popular writers of the last 250 years, including: Bram Stoker, the gothic novelist; Washington Irving, the essayist and short story writer; Charles Mackay, the journalist; Adam Smith, the economist; and Voltaire, the enlightenment writer, historian and philosopher.

ALSO AVAILABLE FROM NEWTON PAGE

A Full and Impartial Account of the Company of Mississipi: Otherwise call'd the French East-India-Company, Projected and settled by Mr. Law

Anonymous

ISBN-13: 978-1-934619124

First published anonymously in London during the height of John Law's Mississippi Scheme. The first ever stock market boom created by John Law's Mississippi Scheme induced significant political and financial resentment throughout Europe. Detractors sought to damage the Mississippi Company by commissioning propagandist pamphlets which undermined the reputation of the company, and created instability among its existing and potential investors. In an attempt to counter such damage, and to both restore the reputation of the Mississippi Scheme and dismiss the predictions of its impending demise, the Mississippi Company released A Full and Impartial Account of the Company of Mississipi.

ALSO AVAILABLE FROM NEWTON PAGE

Thomas Mun, The Complete Works: Economics and Trade

Thomas Mun

ISBN-13: 978-1-934619117

Contains both Mun's earliest work, 'A Discourse of Trade from England unto the East Indies' (1621) which first revealed his mercantilist ideas on economics and trade to the public, and also his hugely influential second work, 'England's Treasure by Foreign Trade' (1664) which developed those ideas, became known as the gospel of finance and commercial policy, and ruled the economic policies of Europe for over a century. Thomas Mun (1571-1641) was a successful merchant, and a director of the East India Company. Probably the most well known of the mercantilist writers, he is also considered to be one of the most enlightened.

ALSO AVAILABLE FROM NEWTON PAGE

The Chimera: Or, The French Way of Paying National Debts Laid Open

Daniel Defoe

ISBN-13: 978-1-934619100

First published anonymously in 1720, Daniel Defoe's *The Chimera: Or, The French Way of Paying National Debts Laid Open* is a prophetic exposé, critique and damnation of John Law's Mississippi Scheme. As one of the cornerstones of investigative financial journalism, *The Chimera* is testament to Defoe's remarkable insight into the European economic crises of the 1720s. His contemporary dissection of the euphoria and excesses of the first ever stock market boom unleashed by John Law and the Mississippi Scheme betrays a striking prescience unequalled by any other writer of the time. A classic propagandist pamphlet deliberately crafted to create uncertainty among the Mississippi Company investors, it correctly predicted, and helped bring about, the imminent demise of the Mississippi Scheme.

ALSO AVAILABLE FROM NEWTON PAGE

The Memoirs Life and Character of the Great Mr. Law and His Brother at Paris

Gray

ISBN-13: 978-1-934619094

First published in London soon after the collapse of John Law's Mississippi Scheme, and his escape from Paris to Venice. Gray claims to have been personally acquainted with John Law from the time Law first left Scotland until the time he was forced to leave France. As a writer employed by Law in his Parisian comptoir during the period in which he was Controller General of France, Gray provides a first-hand account of many aspects of the rise and fall of both Law and his Mississippi Scheme. This pamphlet remains an important and influential contemporary narrative of both the life of John Law and his Mississippi Scheme, and the accounts it contains have been used as source material for all subsequent biographies of John Law.

ALSO AVAILABLE FROM NEWTON PAGE

Letters to John Law

A Letter to Mr. Law
The Case of Mr. Law Truly Stated
A Second Letter to Mr. Law

Selected and introduced by

Gavin John Adams

ISBN-13: 978-1-934619087

This collection of three uncompromising early eighteenth-century propagandist pamphlets documents the wildly contrasting reactions to Law's surprise return to Britain. Crafted by the most prominent journalists, commentators and political agitators of the day, each provides an invaluable contemporaneous social, political and historical record of the most remarkable story in financial history.

ALSO AVAILABLE FROM NEWTON PAGE

John Law and the Mississippi Scheme:

An Anthology

Daniel Defoe

ISBN-13: 978-1-934619070

Daniel Defoe is the father of economic and financial journalism. This anthology is testament to his remarkable insight into the European economic crises of the 1720s. His contemporary accounts of the euphoria and excess of the first ever stock market boom unleashed by John Law and his Mississippi Scheme, and the despair and poverty that followed its crash betray a chilling prescience and an unyielding strength of conviction that very few journalists have possessed since. *John Law and the Mississippi Scheme: An Anthology*, includes: The Chimera (1720), The Case of Mr. Law Truly Stated (1721), and Selected Journalism (1719-1722).

ALSO AVAILABLE FROM NEWTON PAGE

The Mississippi Bubble

A Memoir of John Law

Adolphe Thiers

ISBN-13: 978-1934619056

An established classic and authoritative historical analysis of the spectacular rise and fall of the most enigmatic genius in financial and economic history. It provides a compelling biographical narrative of John Law's life, a considered examination of his Mississippi Scheme, and enlightening accounts of both the Darien Expedition and South Sea Bubble.

ALSO AVAILABLE FROM NEWTON PAGE

The Financier Law

His Scheme and Times: A Graphic Description of the Origin, Maturity and Wreck of the Mississippi Scheme

André Cochut

ISBN-13: 978-1934619049

A richly contextual narrative of the life of John Law, a charismatic Scottish economist and murderer and who would escape execution and use his seemingly effortless financial genius to rise from obscurity to become the most powerful member of the French court, the controller of the French economy, and the richest man the modern world had ever seen.

ALSO AVAILABLE FROM NEWTON PAGE

John Law of Lauriston

Financier and Statesman, Founder of the Bank of France, Originator of the Mississippi Scheme

A. W. Wiston-Glynn

ISBN-13: 978-1934619032

The true story of a Scottish murderer, philanderer, gambler and abscondee who escaped his condemned cell in London to become the darling of the French economy, John Law of Lauriston is an account of the euphoria and wealth Law created by engineering the first stock market boom, and the despair, poverty and destruction which followed its inevitable crash.

ALSO AVAILABLE FROM NEWTON PAGE

The Life of John Law

Including a Detailed Account of the Rise, Progress and Termination of the Mississippi System

John Phillip Wood

ISBN-13: 978-1934619018

One of the most cited biographies of John Law in existence. It is both a concise and gripping retelling of the extraordinary life story of the 'first millionaire' and also a very readable and entertaining account of the remarkably swift rise and even swifter decline of both of his influential innovations: the Mississippi Company and the Mississippi Scheme.

Made in the USA
Las Vegas, NV
02 April 2026

44647529R00031